The Divine Drama of Love

by
James A. Fowler

Edited by
Sylvia Burnett

C.I.Y. PUBLISHING
P.O. BOX 1822
FALLBROOK, CALIFORNIA 92088-1822
www.christinyou.net

THE DIVINE DRAMA OF LOVE

Published by
C.I.Y. PUBLISHING
P.O. BOX 1822
FALLBROOK, CALIFORNIA 92088-1822

www.christinyou.net

ISBN 978-1-929541-17-1

Printed in the United States of America

EDITOR'S NOTE

Jim Fowler, a contemporary theologian with remarkable insight into the heart of Christianity, has devoted most of his sixty-some years to sharing the message that **the Spirit of Christ indwells every Christian.** Echoing the words of the apostle Paul, Mr. Fowler asks, "Do you not realize that Christ is in you?" (II Cor. 13:5).

In this unique dramatic reading the author reveals the "how" and "why" of a spirit-being indwelling mankind ... and, in characteristic form, he leads his readers once again to the heart of Christianity: "Christ in you, the hope of glory" (Col. 1:27).

In this edited version, detailed theological explanations have been condensed in order to allow the overall story to flow more smoothly. (Readers desiring to peruse the fully extended text can find it in the recently published volume entitled *Theo-Drama*, a part of the Christocentric Theology series.)

May this book bring peace and joy to all those who read it. And most importantly, may it bring glory to the eternal triune God, our Savior.

Sylvia Burnett
January, 2009

CONTENTS

Introduction 1

ACT ONE 3

ACT TWO 7

ACT THREE 13
    Scene 1
    Scene 2
    Scene 3

ACT FOUR 25
    Scene 1
    Scene 2

ACT FIVE 37
    Scene 1
    Scene 2

ACT SIX 45
    Scene 1
    Scene 2
    Scene 3
    Scene 4

ACT SEVEN 65

Curtain Call 71

ƗNƮ₹⊙ĐỰ₡ƮƗ⊙N

The Divine Drama of Love dates back to antiquity—before time began, actually—and it continues to be played out around the world. As the title implies, God is the One Who wrote the script for the Drama. It is important, however, to recognize that God is not just the *playwright*. He is also the *director* of the Drama—the One Who tells people where to go, how to perform, etc. And furthermore, He is the *lead actor*. He is the hero of the story. It is HIS story, and as "His story" it is "history"—not only in past tense, but also in present and future.

Many people will acknowledge God's role as "creative genius" of the Drama, but they may wonder—as the world rages around us!—whether God is still taking an active part in the Drama. Fear not! God is still actively involved.

If we say that God is detached or separated from the action of the Drama, the Drama becomes but a spontaneous humanistic improvisation in the context of a deistic detachment, in which God is neither the playwright, nor the director, nor the lead actor, but simply a *spectator* to the humanistic experiment. Such is not the case, however. God continues to be fully involved—as playwright, director, and lead actor of the Divine Drama.

Since "God is Love" (I John 4:8,16), the Drama is a "love story". Granted, there is much action and adventure. There is mystery and tragedy. There is even what some might consider "sci-fi" because it is supernatural. But above all, it is a "love story"—The Divine Drama of Love.

ACT ONE

[The lead character of the Drama—God, the divine Lover—is introduced.]

"In the beginning God ... " (Gen. 1:1). Thus begins the Biblical narrative.

Very often, theologians begin "HIS-story" with God making a plan, determining precepts and laws, making decrees, predetermining events, electing this person or that person. But the reality is simpler than that.

It is not that "In the beginning God ... was studying His moves over a big chess board."

Not, "In the beginning God ... was planning a cosmic biological or social experiment."

Not, "In the beginning God ... laid out the laws of the universe and of behavior, and then sat down in the heavenly courtroom on the Judge's bench to enact justice concerning the performance of the laws."

Not, "In the beginning God … picked the petals of a daisy, and said, 'I love him; I love him not.' "

The script for the Divine Drama of Love begins with God Himself. "In the beginning God …" The Drama begins with Who God *is*, rather than with what God does or has done … for God *does* what He *does*, because He *is* Who He *is*.

Obviously, God is personal. He is a totally unique Person. There is only one God. And "God is Love." This is not to say that God *has* some love to dispense. God is not giving out "love potion number 9". God *is* Love, inherent in Himself.

There is only one God … and yet, there are three Persons. God is the relational three-in-one Trinity of Father, Son, and Holy Spirit. Among the three Persons of God there is (and always has been and always will be) a perfect and ultimate relationship of Love. God is the essence of all proper and perfect interpersonal relationships.

The very essence of God is Love. By definition, love cannot be passive; it must be dynamically expressed to another. The concept of love requires at least two persons, so that love may flow from one to the other. Thus, "God is Love" demands and necessitates that God is a plurality—that there is "otherness" in the oneness of God. Among the Father and the Son and the Holy Spirit, love is constantly flowing from one to the other.

The Divine Drama of Love begins with the existence of God. The New Testament record confirms this beginning, and defines the one God as a plurality. (The Biblical narrative does not always present events in chronological order. Additional insights are sometimes revealed later in the text, as in this case.) In the Gospel of John we read:

> In the beginning was the Word (the Person of God the Son), and the Word was with God (the Father), and the Word was God. He was in the beginning with God. (John 1:1-2)

The "Being" of God, however, is not just static existence. God's Being of Love is continually *expressed* in action. And likewise, God's action is always expressive of His Being of Love. There is an abundance of action in the Divine Drama; and whenever there is action, it is God in the action ... not just the person doing or performing the action. God is intimately involved in every act and action of the Divine Drama.

The sole issue of Act One is the activity of God's own Being of Love, prior to any creative activity. How long does Act One last? It goes on forever, since God is eternal. Act One does not terminate with a curtain before the subsequent Acts of the Drama. The Love of God goes on and on, forever and ever.

ACT TWO

"In the beginning God created the heavens and the earth" (Gen. 1:1).

Creation is *ek theos*, "out of God", for God is the source and origin of all things. The philosophical viewpoint of creation *ex nihilo*, "out of nothing", doesn't "play" well in the Divine Drama. All one gets from nothing is nothing.

In this beginning creative stage of the Drama, the issue is not "things" anyway. The material realm is just the "stage" for the Drama. It becomes a theatre of the absurd when those who are supposed to participate in the Drama spend all of their time arguing about how the stage was built, or how to properly care for it. It's truly a sad phenomenon when environmentalists deify the "stage"—idolizing the physical environment they seek to protect—rather than focusing on the Creator and the Drama of God's Love.

In Act One the sole issue is God, and God's character of Love. In Act Two the issue is expanded to "others". God created others so that they too might participate in His interaction of relational Love. That is what divine Love does! Love wants to draw others into the joy and love of the triune relationship of God.

"God created the heavens and the earth ..." When we read this phrase, we think of the earth beneath our feet and the vast universe of sky and stars, as well as planets and galaxies beyond our gaze. The phrase "the heavens and the earth" is broad enough to include heavenly beings or angelic beings, as well. Such creatures are not specifically mentioned in the first chapter of Genesis, but they are referred to elsewhere in scripture, as we shall see. God created a "heavenly host" of "others"—spirit beings that could participate in the Trinitarian Love relationship. These heavenly/angelic beings were created with freedom of choice, since love cannot be forced or coerced. They were free to receive and enjoy God's Love, or to spurn and reject it.

The angel Lucifer, the "light-bearer", chose to spurn God's Love. The details of the story are not given in the Genesis account, as God did not see fit to begin "HIS-story" with the details of angelic betrayal and divorce, but the story can be found elsewhere in the scriptural record:

> Isa. 14:12-15 (KJV) — How thou art fallen from heaven, O Lucifer, son of the morning! How thou art cut down to the ground, which didst weaken the nations! For thou hast said in thine heart, I will ascend into heaven, I will exalt my throne above the stars of God: I will sit also upon the mount of the congregation, in the sides of the north: I will ascend above the heights of the clouds; I will be like the most High. Yet thou shalt be brought down to hell, to the sides of the pit.

> II Pet. 2:4 — God did not spare angels when they sinned, but cast them into hell and committed them to pits of darkness, reserved for judgment.

> Jude 6 — And angels who did not keep their own domain, but abandoned their proper abode, He has kept in eternal bonds under darkness for the judgment of the great day.

The imagery of Lucifer's great betrayal of God's Love is captured by John Milton in his classic of English literature, *Paradise Lost:*

Author of evil, unknown till thy revolt ...
How hast thou disturbed
Heaven's blessed peace, and unto Nature brought
Misery, uncreated till the crime
Of thy rebellion. How hast thou instilled
Thy malice into thousands, once upright
And faithful, now proved false ...
Heaven casts thee out.

Lucifer, the "light-bearer", who was created
to bear the Light and Love of God Himself,
became Satan, the devil, the Evil One—by
choosing to reject the Love of God. What
prompted him to reject God's Love? Where did
he come up with such an idea? We do not know.
This is the great puzzle of theodicy (i.e., an
understanding of the origin of evil and all that is
contrary to God's nature).

The angel Lucifer was not tempted by
another being; therefore, his rejection of God's
Love was not the *derivation* of evil from another,
but the *origination* of evil. By Lucifer's choice to
spurn the Love of God, to attempt to become "like
the Most High God" (a "power-trip"), he became
the origin and personification of all self-oriented
evil. He became the opposite of Love: selfishness.

Lucifer had the "I-disease"—"I will be like the Most High God."

In reality, what Lucifer did was to call into question the very character of God ... to question God's Love and to deny that it was unconditional, unselfish, and totally other-oriented. "God does not love like that," Lucifer asserted. "God is selfish! God is holding something back from us." And he persuaded a host of other heavenly beings to join him in the rejection of God's Love.

Thus, Act Two draws to a close. We have seen God's Love expressed as He "created the heavens and the earth" ... and also, we have seen God's Love spurned and rejected by Lucifer and other angelic beings. There was a betrayal ... and a great divorce took place. But this was an important part of the Drama, as the "necessary opposite" was introduced.

ACT THREE

Scene 1

"In the beginning God created man ... male and female created He them" (Gen. 1:26,27).

Some theologians have suggested that God created man because He was lonely, or because "He needed someone to hang with." But such is not the case. God is perfect Love in Trinity—with an abundance of love constantly flowing from one to the other among the Father, Son, and Holy Spirit. God is complete in Himself. He doesn't *need* anything!

If God created man because He needed someone else to fulfill Himself, then God's well-being is contingent on man! NEVER! God created man because He desired that "others" participate in the love-fest of His Trinitarian Love.

But love always involves risk! Some of the first created "others" rejected God's Love. Why, then, would He risk creating another kind of "others"—human beings—also with freedom of choice? It was definitely risky! But God took the risk of creating mankind *by* His Love and *for* His Love. It might be said that God's greatest limitation is that He has Self-limited Himself to love His created "others" without overriding their freedom of choice to respond. They are free to receive and enjoy His Love or to spurn it.

There is such *freedom* in true love! Genuine love is not controlling or manipulative. It allows the other person to respond in the way he/she chooses to respond. But, in freedom is risk! The love might be rejected!

Though God had been spurned by some of the angelic heavenly beings, He did not create mankind "on the rebound" or as a "replacement" for the rebellious angels. God's creation of man was not a "Plan B" substitution. He knew from eternity past that He would create mankind to participate in His triune Love—to be His beloved

14

ones. The apostle Paul made this clear in his epistle to the Ephesians (1:3-10).

> Long before He laid down earth's foundation, He had us in mind, had settled on us as the focus of His love, to be made whole and holy by His love. Long, long ago he decided to adopt us into His family through Jesus Christ. (What pleasure He took in planning this!) He wanted us to enter into the celebration of His lavish gift-giving by the hand of His beloved Son.
>
> ... Long before we first heard of Christ and got our hopes up, He had His eye on us, had designs on us for glorious living. (*The Message* – Eugene Peterson)

Because God "had us in mind, had settled on us as the focus of His love," He created mankind with the capacity to participate in His Love in a manner in which no other part of the created order was capable. Even the angelic "others" that God created were originally intended to assist in the special relationship of love between God and man. And all of those "others", both good and evil, do just that—just as God intended.

Scene 2

When God created Adam and Eve, He placed them in a perfect garden, as sort of a wedding present. But guess who showed up at God's "place" in the wedding garden?

Yes, Mr. I-centered Satan wanted center stage in the Drama. This was no surprise to God, for He had purposed to allow Satan to have the "bit-part" of being the necessary opposite so that mankind would have a real choice between two alternatives—between God Who loved them, and Satan, the enemy of God.

In Satan's first encounter with mankind, in the guise of a serpent in the Garden of Eden, he used an approach that was consistent with his own downfall. Satan intimated to man that he should question the character of God's Love and goodness. "If God is really good … If God really loves you … why won't He let you partake of 'the tree of the knowledge of good and evil'? Is there something God doesn't want you to know? What is God holding back on you?" he suggested. Boldly Satan asserted, "Surely you will not die. God just wants to control you. You need to take things into your own hands and experience the fullness of this world. You can control your own life."

Satan lied to the first couple, offering them a pseudo-power to run their own lives instead of following God's script and participating in God's Love. Satan was attempting to ruin the Divine Drama of Love!

Satan—as the illicit, false lover (with the character of evil and self-orientation)—sought to seduce the first human lovers into an adulterous and idolatrous affair. And how did they respond? What did they do? How did they exercise their freedom of choice?

Alas, Adam and Eve kicked off their honeymoon by sleeping with the enemy! They accepted his selfish lies and jumped into bed with him, unaware that he would control them (and all subsequent generations) as "slaves of sin".

Can you imagine how this betrayal must have affected God's heart of love? How would you have felt if your beloved had sneaked out on your honeymoon night and had an illicit affair with a stranger?

Thus, this 2nd scene of Act Three must be entitled "The Fall of Man". As the betrayal is played out on the stage, the air seems to pulse with the pain in God's heart of love.

How would God respond to this betrayal by mankind? If we didn't know God's character of Love, we might think He would be an offended deity, responding with vengeance: "Somebody's going to pay!" Or perhaps He would respond as an exacting Judge, demanding punitive consequence and imposing the death sentence. Or perhaps He would be a vindictive, "get-even" kind of God, sending people to hell and wanting a payment of blood.

But God is Love, a God of LIFE. Yes, death did come upon mankind, as God had said it would if man ate of "the tree of knowledge of good and evil"—but it did not come as God's punishment. "The one having the power of death, that is, the devil" (Heb. 2:14), brought death upon the human race.

God loves mankind, every one of us. He is not against us, nor is He "out to get us" and "make us pay". But He does employ a "tough love" that holds us accountable for our choices.

We must not think of God as a devil who demands his due. We must recognize that death, and hell, and sin, and ungodliness and corruption are derived *ek diabolos*, "out of the devil". They are not to be blamed directly on God.

It grieved God's heart when Adam and Eve rejected His Love, but He respected their choice to do so. He allowed them to unite with the one who is "a liar and the father of lies" (John 8:44). And He allowed Satan, the originator of sin, the "god of this fallen world" (II Cor. 4:4), "the prince of the power of the air", to be the spirit-being who "worked in the sons of disobedience" (Eph. 2:2).

What a sad day that was for God. You see, God had created mankind in a special way, for His own purpose. Man was given not only a

physical body, with a mind, will, and emotion …
but also a spirit, capable of being indwelt by a
spirit-being, so that God Himself could dwell in
the spirit of man and be in constant loving
fellowship with him. Into the spirit of the first
man, Adam, God imparted His own Spirit by
"breathing the breath of life" into him (Gen. 2:7).

But when Adam sinned against God by
rejecting His Love, a calamitous change was
effected in the spiritual relationship between God
and man. The Spirit of God moved out of man's
spirit … allowing Satan to move in, to become the
controlling spirit-being within the spirit of
mankind.

Because of mankind's "original sin" in the
Garden of Eden, God removed His Spirit from
man's spirit. The resulting deprived spiritual
condition of mankind (i.e., the human spirit being
devoid of God's Spirit within) was passed down
to all subsequent generations, from father to
offspring. Every human being ever born has been
born devoid of the Spirit of God … with one

remarkable exception, which shall be seen in the next Act of the Drama.

Scene 3

As the Divine Drama unfolds, Satan's control over the hearts and minds of mankind is grimly evident.

Adam and Eve produced sons Cain and Abel, and when they were grown, Cain killed Abel. Cain derived what he did from the devil, "who was a murderer from the beginning" (John 8:44; I John 3:12). As time went on, the dramas on the side stages got more selfish and more sordid. At one point God's heart was so grieved that He said, "I'm sorry I ever made them" (Gen. 6:6).

Yet, all the time, because God *is* Love, He kept pursuing those He had made for His Love. He chose one family—beginning with Abraham, his son Isaac, and his son Jacob (also known as Israel)—to be an example to all mankind. He gave the Israelite people special instructions (the Law), protected them from their enemies, and performed miracles for their benefit as He rescued them from slavery in Egypt and led them to the Promised Land. Many times the Israelites promised to love God and obey Him, but they were repeatedly unfaithful to Him.

God sent love letters to His chosen people through the prophets, who came voicing God's loving heart in their messages:

> Isaiah 25:6-8 — … the LORD of Hosts will prepare a banquet of rich fare for all the people … the LORD will swallow up that veil that shrouds all the peoples, the pall thrown over all the nations; He will swallow up death forever. Then the LORD God will wipe away the tears from every face and remove the reproach of His people from the whole earth.

> Isaiah 30:18 — … the LORD is waiting to show you His favor; He yearns to have pity on you.

> Isaiah 66:18 — … the time is coming to gather all nations and tongues. And they shall come and see My glory.

> Hosea 11:1-4 — When Israel was a boy, I loved him; I called My son out of Egypt; but the more I called, the further they went from Me; … It was I who taught Ephraim to walk, I who had taken them in My arms; but they did not know … that I led them with bonds of love—that I had lifted them like a little child to My cheek, that I had bent down to feed them.

Hosea 14:4 — I will heal their apostasy; of My own bounty I will love them.

Malachi 1:2 — "I have loved you," says the LORD. But you say, "How hast Thou loved us?"

Malachi 3:13,14 — "You have used hard words about Me," says the LORD, and then you ask, "How have we spoken against Thee?" You have said, "It is useless to serve God; what do we gain from the LORD of Hosts by observing His rules and behaving with deference?" (from last page of Old Testament)

Then there followed 400 years of relative silence. It almost appeared that the curtain had come down on the Divine Drama … that the love relationship was no longer being pursued by God or man.

*** *Intermission* ***

The first three Acts of the Divine Drama of Love have taken us through the old covenant, the Old Testament. But "HIS-story" does not end there. It can't! … or God would cease to be the faithful God of Love, the relentless Lover wanting "others" to participate in His Love. Love is the very essence of God. Thus, He cannot cease to *be* Love, or to *act* in Love.

God had intimated to the first couple in the Garden of Eden that He would come back for them—a Messianic promise (Gen. 3:15) which He renewed throughout the old covenant. And of course, He kept His promise.

What God did to restore the broken love relationship between God and man was so phenomenal, so singularly important in the Divine Drama, that most human calculation of time and history is determined by that action. God's action of Love was the dividing point in human history between B.C. and A.D.; between the Old Testament and the New Testament in the Biblical narrative; between the old covenant and the new covenant that God established with man.

ACT FOUR

Scene 1

Faithful to His promises, the God of Love acted in love to restore His beloved human beings into His Trinitarian Love.

Why did it take so long? Why didn't God act as soon as man rejected His Love there in the Garden of Eden? Why did He exile them from the Garden and wait thousands of years before taking action to restore mankind into His Love?

God was allowing mankind sufficient time to recognize that God's way is the best way. He allowed mankind to learn by life experience. Mankind needed to see that the devil's lie about their being able to run their own lives led only to being "slaves of sin", ruled by Satan. Mankind needed to recognize that self-orientation could never lead to any genuine sense of relationship and community. Even after God gave the Law to the Israelite people, He allowed time for them to learn that the Law could not break the bonds of sin and restore the love relationship between God and man. Only God's Love and grace could do that … could enable mankind to be what he was intended to be, both individually and collectively.

God *loved* mankind. Even though they had rejected His Love, still He longed for them to participate in His Trinitarian Love. But how could He reach them? What more could He do to express His Love to the fallen human beings He had created? What would it take to make them understand how much He loved them?

What God did was wonderful! Marvelous! Truly phenomenal! "In the fullness of time …" —in the providence of God's perfect timing— "God sent forth His Son, born of a woman" (Gal. 4:4). God *loved* the world so much that He gave His own Son (John 3:16).

Not, "God begrudgingly considered the plight of mankind, and sent a representative."

Not, "God determined to engage in a power-play and make things right by sending His right-hand man."

Not, "God decided to assert His authority and use His limitless resources to buy man out of his problem."

God expressed His Love for fallen humanity by sending His own beloved Son—that is, God the Father sent God the Son. The Son went down to earth personally, to tell mankind (and to show them) how much God loved them.

Soren Kierkegaard uses this analogy:

> Suppose there was a king who loved a humble maiden. The king was like no other king. Every statesman trembled before his power. No one dared breathe a word against him, for he had the strength to crush all opponents. And yet this mighty king was melted by love for a humble maiden. How could he declare his love for her? In an odd sort of way, his kingliness tied his hands. If he brought her to the palace and crowned her head with jewels and clothed her body in royal robes, she would surely not resist—no one dared resist him. BUT, would she love him?
>
> She would say she loved him, of course, but would she truly? Or would she live with him in fear, nursing a private grief for the life she had left behind? Would she be happy at his side? How could he know? If he rode to her forest cottage in

his royal carriage, with an armed escort waving bright banners, that too would overwhelm her. He did not want a cringing subject. He wanted a lover, an equal. He wanted her to forget that he was a king and she a humble maiden, and to let shared love cross the gulf between them. For it is only in love that the unequal can be made equal.

So the king clothed himself as a beggar and renounced his throne in order to win her hand.

The analogy breaks down (as all analogies do), but it attempts to express the Love of God for man, and His willingness to become a Man for man.

C. S. Lewis expressed this extraordinary action of God as "the great invasion of God into enemy-occupied territory". Ever since the Fall of man in the Garden of Eden, "the whole world of mankind was held in the power of the Evil One" (I John 5:19). God sent His Son into this enemy-occupied territory, somewhat incognito, disguised as a baby in a manger in Bethlehem. Why did He use this low-key approach? Because God wanted to woo His lovers, not just overcome the world in an omnipotent power-play. Acting 180 degrees opposite of the world's way, God employed the power of weakness, the power of humiliation, the power of Love.

The incarnation (i.e., the act by which God was invested with bodily nature and form) was staged beautifully by God in the Divine Drama. The "silent night", the shepherds watching their flocks out in the fields, the angels who appeared to them, the manger into which the swaddled infant was placed— these are the props, the stage settings, the background music for the real drama that was being acted out in history that night.

Unfortunately, Christian "religion" often reduces that miraculous incarnation event to a simple nativity-drama. But it was far more than that! The incarnation was an extraordinary expression of God's Love. To reach the hearts of fallen mankind, God delivered the message Himself—or, to be more precise: the Person of God the Son, sent by God the Father, delivered the message of Love.

Since there is no divergence of love or intent within the Trinity, the Son, "although He existed in the form of God, did not regard equality with

God a thing to be grasped, but emptied Himself, taking the form of a bond-servant, being made in the likeness of men" (Phil. 2:6,7).

The incarnation of the Son of God as the God-man, the "one mediator between God and man" (I Tim. 2:5), is the singular greatest expression of God's Love. "The Word became flesh" (John 1:14). This was not just a role that the Son played in the Divine Drama. Human flesh was not just a robe or a costume that He assumed to play His part. He actually became one of us—a human being! "God sent His Son in the likeness of sinful flesh" (Rom. 8:3). He walked the mile in our moccasins. He lived out the divine Love-life in human existence.

J. B. Phillips tells the story of "The Visited Planet" where a senior angel is showing a younger angel around the universe, and he points out the planet earth.

> "I want you to watch that one particularly," said the senior angel, pointing with his finger.
>
> "Well, it looks very small and rather dirty to me," said the little angel. "What's special about that one?"

"That," replied his senior solemnly, "is the Visited Planet."

"Visited?" said the little one. "You don't mean visited by … ?"

"Indeed I do. That ball, which I have no doubt looks to you small and insignificant and not perhaps overclean, has been visited by our young Prince of Glory." And at these words he bowed his head reverently.

"But how?" queried the younger one. "Do you mean that our great and glorious Prince, with all these wonders and splendours of His creation, went down in Person to that fifth-rate little ball? Why should He do a thing like that?"

"It isn't for us, "said his senior a little stiffly, "to question His 'whys', except that I must point out to you that He is not impressed by size and numbers, as you seem to be. But that He really went I know, and all of us in Heaven who know anything know that. As to why He became one of them—how else do you suppose He could visit them?"

The little angel's face wrinkled in disgust. "Do you mean to tell me," he said, "that He stooped so low as to become one of those creeping, crawling creatures on that floating ball?"

"I do, and I don't think He would like you to call them 'creeping, crawling creatures' in that tone of voice. For, strange as it may seem to us, He loves them. He went down to visit them to lift them up to become like Him."

The little angel looked blank. Such a thought was almost beyond his comprehension.

31

The Son of God assumed humanity …
became flesh … one of us. God's Love-life was
lived out in a man. "God was, in Christ,
reconciling the world to Himself" (II Cor. 5:19).

God didn't act to bash and smash the world
of mankind for having sinned. God loved us. God
sought us. Simon Tugwell wrote:

> So long as we imagine that it is we who have
> to look for God, we must often lose heart. But it is
> the other way about; He is looking for us. And so
> we can afford to recognize that very often we are
> not looking for God; far from it, we are in full
> flight from him, in high rebellion against him.
> And he knows that and has taken it into account.
> He has followed us into our own darkness; there
> where we thought finally to escape him, we run
> straight into his arms. So we do not have to erect
> a false piety for ourselves, to give us the hope of
> salvation. Our hope is his determination to save
> us, and he will not give in.

John Bunyon described the loving God as
"the hound of heaven" who will do everything
possible without violating our freedom of choice
to draw us to Himself and the Trinitarian
fellowship of Love.

Scene 2

In His earthly form as Man, the Son of God was called Jesus. Jesus was born in Bethlehem, raised in Nazareth, and lived a perfect life. He never sinned … not once!

Of course, Mr. I-centered Satan, the enemy of God, did show up on the stage to tempt the Divine One Who had become Man. The Biblical narrative records several specific instances of temptation. When Jesus was led into the wilderness by the Holy Spirit and remained there for 40 days, the Evil One came and tempted Him three times. Jesus resisted those temptations by quoting scripture to the devil. Satan also tempted Jesus just before He died, as Jesus was enduring excruciating physical pain and public humiliation (a situation the devil undoubtedly thought made Him extremely vulnerable to temptation).

But Jesus never gave in to temptation. Not once! He lived among sinful men and was tempted every day by circumstances and people around Him, as all men are. Throughout Jesus' life He was "tempted in all points as we are, yet without sin" (Heb. 4:15). He was also tempted in ways beyond what we are, for the tempter knew that Jesus was God in the flesh and he tempted Him to deny Who He was—to deny His divine Love, His goodness, His purity—and to act in a selfish manner. But Jesus never yielded to temptation.

Many have asked, "If Jesus was truly a human being, how was He able to live a sinless life?"

Historians document that Jesus was truly a human being. He was born, he lived, and he died. He had all the components of a human being: a physical body, complete with mind, will, and emotion, and a spirit. But Jesus differed from all other human beings in one important way. His father was not a human being, not a descendent of Adam, the first man. His father was God! (Matt. 1:20; Luke 1:35).

All other human beings, as descendents of Adam, have been born with their spirit devoid of the Spirit of God. In contrast, Jesus' human spirit was indwelt by the Spirit of God … and from God's presence within, Jesus drew all that He needed to live a sinless life.

Jesus was constantly aware of the presence of God within Him. He was always attuned to the prompting of God's Spirit. Every moment of every day, Jesus submitted His will to the will of God the Father, allowing the Father to manifest Himself through the God-man, Jesus. As Jesus explained, "The Father *abiding in Me* does His works" (John 14:10).

Jesus spent His earthly life doing what His Father had sent Him to do: to tell mankind how much God loved them, and that God longed for the love relationship between God and man to be restored; and to provide the means by which that restoration could be accomplished.

ACT FIVE

[Tragedy strikes. Treason and murder
occur ... and the victim of the crime
is Jesus, God's beloved Son.]

Scene 1

During the 33 years Jesus lived on earth, "He
went about doing good" (Acts 10:38). But because
He was outspoken about the wrongdoings of the
Jewish religious leaders, they hated Him and
conspired to have Him killed. Jesus was crucified
on a cross. God allowed it to happen. In fact, He
purposed that it would happen.

Many people cannot comprehend the Love of
God in the crucifixion. How could a loving God
allow His Son to be crucified on a cross? What
kind of love is that? Why did Jesus have to die?

God's script called for Jesus to die, to forfeit His life as a substitute for all mankind, to pay the "death penalty" for sin so that all might be forgiven.

But why couldn't God have just issued a blanket amnesty plan for mankind? Why couldn't He have just broadcast His forgiveness from the heavens? Why couldn't God have just said, "Ah, forget it. It wasn't that big of a deal anyway"?

Because to God, it was a big deal! Man had sinned against God, using his freedom of choice to reject God's Love. Admittedly, mankind had been duped and deceived and stolen away by "the one having the power of death, that is, the devil" (Heb. 2:14). But this travesty of misused and abused humanity—seduced into slavery to sin, controlled by Satan, overcome by death—could be remedied only by the powerful Love of God, through the death of God's Son.

The Son knew why His Father had sent Him to earth as the God-man. Jesus said, "The Son of Man did not come to be served, but to serve, and to give His life a ransom for many" (Matt. 20:28).

"The Son of God appeared for this purpose, that He might destroy the works of the devil" (I John 3:8). "Through death, He rendered powerless him who had the power of death, that is, the devil" (Heb. 2:14).

There was a cosmic conflict: Satan, the "god of this world" (II Cor. 4:4) with his sin character and death power, reigned over mankind. The Son of God came to earth as a man, willing to submit to death, in order to overcome death and show the impotency of Satan's power ... willing to be "made sin" (II Cor. 5:21) that we might have His life and righteousness. "He gave Himself for our sins, that He might deliver us out of this present evil age" (Gal. 1:4) and "set us free from the yoke of slavery" (Gal. 5:1).

Jesus loved us so much that He was willing to pay the "price", to "taste death for everyone" (Heb. 2:9), to become "the one for the many" (the sacrificial substitute), "delivered up for us all" (Rom. 8:31). Even before the Son of God came to earth, He knew that the incarnation was for the purpose of crucifixion. He did it for love. "He loved us, and gave Himself for us" (Gal. 2:20; Eph. 5:25).

In Jesus' last moments on the cross, He cried out, *"Tetelestai"*, "It is finished!" That was not a cry of defeat, meaning, "It's over! We made a valiant attempt but we failed."

Nor was it a cry of resignation, meaning, "It's done. I'm glad that's over."

Jesus' cry from the cross was a declaration of victory! "It is finished! The battle is won! God's end objective to overcome Satan, death and sin has been accomplished. God's restorative love action to draw all men unto Himself has been set in motion. It cannot fail."

God the Father allowed His beloved Son to suffer the terrible death of crucifixion in order to give mankind a new chance ... a new life! ... a new opportunity to participate in the joy and love of His Trinitarian Love.

Isaac Watts captured the idea of God's Love in the crucifixion in his famous hymn, "When I Survey the Wondrous Cross":

When I survey the wondrous cross,
On which the Prince of glory died,
My richest gain I count but loss,
And pour contempt on all my pride.

See, from His head, His hands, His feet,
Sorrow and *love* flow mingled down;
Did e'er such *love* and sorrow met,
Or thorns compose so rich a crown?

Were the whole realm of nature mine,
That were a present far too small;
Love so amazing, so divine,
Demands my soul, my life, my all.

If the Divine Drama had ended with the death of Jesus, then Jesus would be historically recognized as a martyr, along with Che Gueverra and Martin Luther King, and the only impact of His life and death would be that a religion was established to honor His Name and memorialize His teachings.

If Jesus' death on the cross were the end of the story, then …

• there was a negative without a positive;

• there was a remedial action that remedied the problem of sin without a restorative action that restored man to full relationship with God's Love;

• there was a defeat of self-oriented death without a victory of the divine Love-life for the "others" of mankind.

If Jesus' death on the cross were the end of the story, then the Drama would be left dangling with the tragic death of its hero, without a proper conclusion.

But Jesus' death was not the end of the Divine Drama of Love. God, Who always acts true to His character of Love, took the Drama into yet another realm.

Scene 2

On the third day after Jesus' crucifixion, God raised Jesus from the dead! The Perfect Man, the sinless Savior, the only begotten Son of God could not be held by death. The "one having the power of death, that is, the devil" (Heb. 2:14), had no right to hold Jesus, for He was never connected to or united with Satan, the one having the "power of death". As Jesus explained to His Disciples,

"… the ruler of this world … has nothing in Me"
(John 14:30). Therefore, in submitting to death on
behalf of the "others" of mankind, "it was
impossible for Him to be held in death's power"
(Acts 2:14).

After Jesus' resurrection, He appeared at
various places in the region for several weeks.
Then He ascended into heaven in a cloud,
returning to the glories of the heavenly realm
from which He had come. His work on earth was
done.

ACT SIX

Jesus' resurrection from the dead and His ascension into heaven opened the way for a new kind of life for mankind—resurrection-life!

Scene 1

At long last, God had provided a way for the spiritual relationship between God and man to be restored, a means by which God's Spirit could be restored as the indwelling spirit-being within the human spirit. Any person who believed Jesus to be the Son of God and opened their heart to Him would be filled with the Spirit of God—Father, Son, and Holy Spirit—and Satan would be expelled. The loving spiritual relationship that God originally intended would be restored.

A new kind of life—resurrection-life—is produced by the dynamic (the energy / activity /

power) of Jesus' own Being indwelling the spirit of a person. The indwelling Spirit of Christ is the *empowerment* of the resurrection-life. The apostle Paul understood that, and declared that he desired only "to know Him (the risen Lord Jesus) and the *power* of His resurrection …" (Phil. 3:10).

Jesus promised this empowerment of life to His Disciples when He said, "… you will receive power when the Holy Spirit has come upon you" (Acts 1:8). He was referring to the occasion of Pentecost, 50 days after His death, when believers from all nations were "filled with the Holy Spirit" (Acts 2:4).

Contemporary Christians often view that first-century Pentecost experience simply as the occasion when God distributed spiritual gifts. Christians today tend to regard spiritual gifts as "trophies" of spirituality, or "power toys" for performing Christian ministry, without any integral connection to the living Lord Jesus. They fail to recognize the true significance of Pentecost, as the chronological and historical "beginning" (Acts 11:15) of the restored spiritual relationship of God with all mankind, when the Spirit of Christ was poured out to dwell in the spirit (cf. Rom. 8:16) of those receptive to God's Love.

Every Christian has the Spirit of Christ indwelling his spirit. The apostle Paul explained, "If any man does not have the Spirit of Christ, he is none of His ... but if the Spirit of Him who raised Jesus from the dead dwells in you, He who raised Jesus from the dead will also give life to your mortal bodies through His Spirit who indwells you" (Rom. 8:9-11).

Scene 2

Because God earnestly desires for all mankind to participate in a relationship of love with Him, He offers His Love-life freely to all mankind, to be accepted or rejected by each person. God's Love-life cannot be earned, merited, or purchased—nor is God interested in any kind of trade or transaction with us. The divine Lover does not want any "thing" we might offer Him—whether it be service, dedication, commitment, obedience, sacrifice, moral conformity, etc. God desires only the availability of our hearts and lives, so that He can pour in His Love and the complete sufficiency of His grace.

We must be careful not to get sidetracked by Christian "religion" which insists on our "saying" or "doing" something, rather than the simple availability of our hearts. Through the prophet Isaiah, God expressed His disapproval of actions devoid of heart devotion:

> Because this people draw near with their words, and honor Me with their lip service, but they remove their hearts far from Me, and their reverence for Me consists of tradition learned by rote, therefore behold, I will once again deal marvelously with this people, wondrously marvelous; and the wisdom of their wise men shall perish, and the discernment of their discerning men shall be concealed. (Isaiah 29:13,14)

God is gracious, and patient, and always willing to reveal to men what does not work, so that they will appreciate His provision of the only thing that *will* fulfill man's needs and desires— Himself. God knows what mankind needs most;

man needs God, indwelling his human spirit and giving him "life".

When Nicodemus, a Jewish leader, came to Jesus by night, seeking a fuller understanding of the relationship between God and man, Jesus explained to him, "You must be born again" (John 3:7). He was speaking of spiritual re-birth (also known as spiritual regeneration) whereby the Spirit of God is "born again" in man, i.e., brought to life again in man's spirit.

Spiritual regeneration is not merely a readjustment of our thought processes; it is not simply a reorientation of our desires and aspirations; it is not just a renewal of dedication to be the best we can be. Spiritual regeneration means "to re-life" or "to bring into being again" spiritually. Spiritual re-birth occurs when the Spirit of God is restored within the spirit of a receptive individual, enabling that person to participate in a love relationship with God—just as God intended when He created mankind.

"How can a person be 'born again'?" asked Nicodemus. The concept confused him, and continues to confuse people who are seeking God even today. How can a person be born again? By choice ... by choosing God. Choosing God is called "faith". Faith is not just believing certain doctrines or ideas, nor is it just trusting or relying on what cannot be proved. Faith is the conscious decision to choose God ... to open one's heart to Him, to be receptive to His presence and activity in one's life. When a person has done that—and continues, day by day, to be available to God and receptive to His Spirit—then he/she is a born-again believer and a participant in the Divine Drama of Love.

As the apostle Paul explained to the first-century Ephesians: "For by grace (i.e., God's Love in action) you are saved through *faith* (your intentional choice of believing in Jesus as God's Son and choosing God), that not of yourselves, it is the gift of God; not as a result of works, lest anyone should boast" (Eph. 2:8,9).

When a receptive heart chooses God and begins to participate in His Love-life, that person is "made safe" from enslavement and death in the

Evil One. The process is called "salvation". We are "made safe" from Satan's dysfunctionality in order to function as God intended, to be controlled by the dynamic of His Spirit indwelling our spirit. In salvation we are "made safe" to participate in a love relationship with God.

HAVE YOU MADE THE CHOICE OF FAITH and become a participant in the Divine Drama of God's Love? No one has to remain a spectator in the theatre of life, controlled by Satan and his self-serving lies. God's earnest desire is that every person should become a participant in His Love. "God is not willing that any should perish, but for all to come to repentance" (II Pet. 3:9). Repentance is a "change of mind" that allows for a "change of action"—allowing the Spirit of God to become the dynamic in your life instead of Satan.

When we make the choice of faith—to open our heart to Him and receive His Spirit into our spirit—"the love of God is poured into our hearts through the Holy Spirit Who is given to us" (Rom. 5:10). "The Spirit bears witness with our spirit that we are a child of God" (Rom. 8:16). We are "in Christ"—literally, in *union with* Christ, as His Spirit indwells/resides within our spirit— and we become a "new creature" (II Cor. 5:17), a "new man" (Eph. 4:24; Col. 3:10), participating in God's Love.

As participants in the Divine Drama, the very reality of God's Love and life are being played out *in, as,* and *through* our lives.

If you have not yet opened your heart to God, won't you do so now? Choose God. Accept His Love and the new life He offers.

Scene 3

The Divine Drama does not fade out into eternal bliss after a person chooses to participate in God's Love. Ahead lies a very action-packed adventure, the Christian life. Those who believe in Jesus as the Son of God are called Christians because they are in Christ—"in *union with* Christ" as His Spirit indwells their spirit.

The Christian life is not like a trip to "Fantasyland" at Disneyland, or membership in a "red-carpet club". Becoming a Christian does not ensure that everything will be "coming up roses" in our lives from then on. Life is still filled with joys and sorrows, family obligations, work responsibilities, mishaps, stress, etc. ... and through it all, we continue to be responsible for exercising our freedom of choice. But as Christians, we have the indwelling Spirit of God to help us!

Whenever we are faced with a decision, we have two choices. We can be receptive to the prompting of the indwelling Spirit Who encourages us to walk in the path of righteousness, or we can listen to the seductive voice of the serpent that slithers nearby and attempts to lead us into paths of selfishness.

Satan, who always wants center stage, ever seeks to disrupt God's Drama of Love. The Evil One is constantly "prowling around like a roaring lion, seeking someone to devour" (I Pet. 5:8), figuratively firing "flaming arrows" (Eph. 6:16), and attempting to "lure" Christians back into selfish desires (James 1:14). Satan will do everything he can to diminish a Christian's participation in God's Love.

As "accuser of the brethren" (Rev. 12:10), Satan tries to make us doubt that we have been spiritually reborn and transformed into a new creature in Christ. "So," he taunts, "you think you've been made righteous? Just look at your behavior. Is that righteousness?" Or he seeks to cause us to doubt God's Love. "What makes you think God loves you? If God loves you, why are you having so many problems in your life?"

Unfortunately, there *are* troubles and hardships in this earthly life, and there may be times when we doubt God's Love. Or there may be times when we are unable to forgive ourselves for wrong choices, and we find it hard to believe that God could love someone who has done what we have done. We must simply "keep on believing", as we cry unto Him, "Lord, help my unbelief!" (Mark 9:24).

God loves us. (Remember, His very essence is Love. He cannot stop *being* Love or *acting* in Love.) God loves us and has promised to be with us always, and He is faithful to help us overcome all of Satan's assaults (his suggestions that we are a fraud, a failure, a hopeless sinner) and all of Satan's attempts to create anxiety, shame, insecurity, and condemnation. The indwelling "Helper" is ever present to reassure our doubting hearts, to encourage us, and to strengthen our faith.

One of Satan's foremost temptations is to try to get us to settle for the external regimen of "religion" instead of the internal love relationship of joy and peace that we enjoy by participating in the Divine Drama of Love. The tempter would substitute a regimen of repetitious order, an obligatory list of rules and regulations, full of "oughts" and "shoulds" of behavioral performance. "You should read your Bible more, pray more, go to church more, give more money," the devil admonishes (often while dressed in the garb of a preacher). Satan wants us to accept the bondage of "religion" so we'll be too busy "playing church" to have time to *be* God's beloved, to be receptive to His activity in our lives and to participate in His Love.

All Christians succumb at times to the spiritual adultery of outward forms of "religion". But Christianity is not "religion". Christianity is not a system of propositions to be assented to and adhered to. Christianity is not rituals and traditions of the institutional church. Christianity is Christ!—the risen, living Lord indwelling the spirit of every Christian.

Christians are "new creatures", made for a loving relationship with God. When they redirect their focus from God to "religion", they begin to feel restless, empty and lonely. The shallowness of the status-quo of "religion" causes them to ask, "Is that all there is?" Too many Christians, wounded by the false love of "religion", think that the objective of the Christian life is "survival" in this world, instead of the excitement of a love relationship with God. Satan is delighted, of course, whenever he can divert a Christian's attention away from God.

As Christians we sometimes yield to the devil's suggestions and solicitations. As a result, we manifest sinful behavior expressive of the character of Satan rather than righteous behavior expressive of the character of Christ. When we sin, we misrepresent who we are in Christ; we act "out of character".

We are sometimes surprised that we must continue to contend with deep-seated issues of selfishness and addictive patterns of the "flesh". The devil is quick to suggest to us that perhaps our identity in Christ is not secure. But we do not have to be disheartened by his lies. We need only go to our divine Lover and confess, "I cannot seem to overcome this; only You can. My desire is to let You do so." And He is faithful to forgive our sins (I John 1:9) and to provide strength to overcome.

The apostle Paul explained that "no temptation has overtaken you but such as is common to man; and God is faithful, Who will not allow you to be tempted beyond what you are able, but with the temptation will provide the way of escape also, that you may be able to endure it" (I Cor. 10:13). The living Lord Jesus "is able to come to the aid of those who are tempted" (Heb. 2:18). "Greater is He Who is in you than he who is in the world" (I John 4:4). We are "protected by the power of God" (I Pet. 1:5).

God is not unaware that we have trials in this life. These trials are the circumstances and situations in which the tempter *tempts*, while at the same time God *tests* us. The words "tempt" and "test" in the New Testament are the same Greek word (*peirazo*); the appropriate translation of the word is determined by the character of the spirit who is soliciting the action. Satan *tempts* us, wanting us to express his selfish character of sinfulness. God *tests* us in order to ascertain whether we will rely on the provision of His grace in the midst of the difficulties. Even the Evil One serves God's purposes, for in the tempting-versus-testing alternative, we are given a genuine choice. With each temptation, we can submit to

Satan and his evil intentions or we can submit ourselves to God and His good and perfect plan for our lives.

Faith is the key. In all situations, we have a choice—God or Satan. Choose God! Live by faith! "As you received Christ Jesus (by faith), so walk in Him" (Col. 2:6).

While Satan continues to harass us, "in all these things we overwhelmingly conquer through Him Who loved us ... convinced that nothing shall be able to separate us from the love of God which is in Christ Jesus our Lord" (Rom. 8:37-39).

Scene 4

God desires for the JOY of the Lord to be experienced by every Christian. With the Spirit of Christ indwelling us, we are meant to live in wonder and joy. This *joy* is not the same as *happiness*. Happiness is based on the happenstances of life and whether we find them pleasant or unpleasant. Joy, on the other hand, is the appreciation of God's Love and grace in the midst of any circumstance.

The divine Love-life that the Christian receives in Christ (in *union with* Christ) is not just a deposit, to be experienced in heaven someday. God's Love-life is meant to enrich our lives in the present as well—as His indwelling Spirit infuses us with joy and peace. But sadly, many Christians are not filled with joy. They seem to be unaware that Christ is in them. The apostle Paul observed this same problem in the first-century, and he asked those less-than-joyful Christians, "Do you not recognize that Jesus Christ is in you?" (II Cor. 13:5).

"This is the mystery ... Christ in you, the hope of glory" (Col. 1:26,27). "It is no longer I who live, but Christ lives in me" (Gal. 2:20). With the Spirit of Christ indwelling every Christian, the Christian life should be characterized by light-heartedness—by "love, joy, peace ..." (Gal. 5:22)—as well as a unique sense of spontaneity, mystery, discovery, adventure, anticipation, freedom, transparency, intimacy, and ecstasy.

God, as playwright of the Divine Drama, does have a prepared script ... but He created each of us as unique individuals, which allows for the spontaneity of unique expression.

"Religion", on the other hand, portrays the Christian life as role-playing in strict accord with the script (the Scripture Book) and "staying in character" by aligning with the rules of the Law. Those who can best memorize their "parts" are then considered the best Christian actors. Unfortunately, that is a tragic misrepresentation of the divine Love-life. God regards such righteous deeds, performed by rote, as but "a filthy rag" (Isaiah 64:6) and "rubbish" (Phil. 3:8) in His sight.

God expects nothing more from us than what He provides for us, enacts in us, and expresses through us. He is the dynamic of His own demands, and the expression of His own expectations. "Love fulfills the law" (Rom. 13:8-10; Gal. 5:14).

"God is Love," and the expression of His divine character of Love is the objective of the

Divine Drama. The apostle John, known as the "apostle of love", wrote these words:

> Beloved, let us love one another, for love is from God; and everyone who loves is born of God and knows God. The one who does not love does not know God, for God is love. (I John 4:7-8)

Jesus said, "By this will all men know that you are My disciples, if you have love for one another" (John 13:35). The apostle Paul wrote, "... the fruit of the Spirit is love ..." (Gal. 5:22). "By their fruit you will know them" (Matt. 7:16), Jesus explained.

The collective social expression of God's Love for "others" is to be found in the church. The church, as a community of love, is meant to express the divine triune community of love—the love constantly flowing among the Father, the Son, and the Holy Spirit.

Loving is the active expression of God's own Being. We, as created beings, are not capable of generating love. Love is not part of our human nature. Only "God *is* Love." Thus, in order for us to express genuine love, we must allow God to express Himself (Love) through us—both in the individual Christian and in the collective expression of interpersonal relationships within the church.

Many Christians mistakenly think that they should try to imitate Christ ... to "live like Jesus" and "love like Jesus" by following His example. However, it is not possible for Christians to be "like Christ" by their own human efforts ... nor is that what Jesus wants us to do. He wants to express His own divine character of Love *in* and *through* our lives—in each of us individually, in a unique way in each of us.

The Christian life is not meant to be
an imitation of the life of Jesus,
but rather a "**manifestation of the life of Jesus
in our mortal bodies**" (II Cor. 4:10,11).

The Christian life can only be lived *by faith*, as we are receptive to God's activity within us ... as we derive and draw all of our thoughts, attitudes, emotions, and actions from the Spirit of God Who indwells us.

ACT SEVEN

Between Acts Two and Three, the Divine Drama crossed the unknown point from the "pre-historical" to the "historical". In similar manner, the Drama now crosses that moving point on the time-line between the "already" and the "not yet", as the fulfillment of God's Drama of Love approaches.

Although we are " complete in Christ" (Col. 2:10) and have already been "blessed with every spiritual blessing in heavenly places" (Eph. 1:3), there is still a "longing for the revealing of the sons of God" (Rom. 8:19). Participants in the divine Love-life "look forward to the joy set before them", convinced that "the sufferings of this present time are not worthy to be compared with the glory that is to be revealed to us" (Rom. 8:18), the "eternal weight of glory far beyond all comparison" (II Cor. 4:17).

Though we have "Christ in us, the hope of glory" (Col. 1:27), there remains an expectation and a desire to be with Him in heaven. Even though we are already participating in the Love-life of the triune God while still physically alive on the earth, there is still the anticipation of the future—as we long to see Him face to face, and look forward to participating in His Love-life forever.

This desire for heaven is not a desire for something *more* than Jesus, Who now indwells us by His Spirit. It is an innate desire for something more than what this physical world offers and inflicts. This world is characterized by discontent and corruption, from which the created order longs to be set free (Rom. 8:19-25).

C. S. Lewis posited the "argument of desire", which briefly stated is: "If I find in myself desires which nothing in this world can satisfy, then the only logical explanation is that I was made for another world." Peter Kreeft made this observation: "If life on earth is not a road to heaven, then it is a treadmill, a merry-go-round minus the merry." The Hebrew philosopher who wrote Ecclesiastes correctly indicated that everything in this world is "vanity", but God "has set eternity in our hearts" (Eccl. 3:11). This is not to say that what one finds in his heart is necessarily heaven, but that there is a heavenly longing in the heart of man that is unsatisfiable by anything on earth. As Peter Kreeft explained, "Heaven is greater than the heart, but can only be discovered by the heart."

There are some who would charge that the hope of heaven is but the wishful thinking of escapism. There may be an escapist mentality among those Christians who fail to realize all that they already have in Jesus Christ, and whose sole focus is on a desire to be snatched away in a "rapture" and delivered from any tribulation. But the desire and expectation of heaven is not necessarily escapist. As Peter Kreeft noted, "Concern for heaven is as escapist as looking through the windshield rather than in the rearview mirror as you are locked in a speeding car lurching over foggy, rocky terrain with no road map." It is important to look in the direction you are going!

Those who would charge "heavenly hope" as being escapist are inevitably those who have no hope! Christian hope is the confident expectation of experiencing all that God has for us. The basis for this hope is Jesus: "Christ Jesus is our hope" (I Tim. 1:1). Having been invited and drawn into participation in the Trinitarian Love relationship, we are "born again to a living hope " (I Pet. 1:3), the hope of continuing that relationship with Him through all eternity.

Jesus comforted Martha on the occasion of the death of her brother Lazarus with these words: "I AM the resurrection and the life; he who believes in Me shall live even if he dies, and everyone who lives and believes in Me shall never die" (John 11:25,26).

There will come a time when, as C. S. Lewis wrote, "the door on which we have been knocking all our lives will open at last." We will cross the threshold out of physical life and continue our walk in the eternal spiritual life of

God's Love. How marvelous that new context of life will be!

All the images we have of heaven are inadequate—even the Biblical images of golden streets, mansions, and crowns. Perhaps the best image of heaven we might employ is that of a "wedding banquet"—the final and forever celebration of the divine Love-life.

"Eye has not seen, nor ear heard, neither has it ever entered into the heart of man, the things which God has prepared for them that love Him" (I Cor. 2:9). Heaven will be a place where the deepest longings of the heart are satisfied, a place devoid of all disappointments and hindrances.

Some people worry that heaven will be boring. There is no need to worry. Heaven is not the monotony of "sitting on a cloud playing a harp" forever. We will "reign with Christ" (II Tim. 2:12; Rev. 20:6) in the eternal kingdom of God, where God will be "all in all" (I Cor. 15:28).

The Divine Drama of Love has a happy ending! But in another sense, there is no ending— for God is eternal and immortal, and His

Trinitarian Love will go on forever. Those of us who have exercised our freedom of choice by choosing God and participating in His Love will share His immortality and participate in the joy of the Love of the Lord forever.

CURTAIN CALL

Inquiring minds want to know, "What about hell?" Some people might think that hell has no part in the Divine Drama, but indeed it has. Everything, and everyone, is part of God's Divine Drama of Love.

God—the Father, Son, and Holy Spirit—*is* Love. He created mankind to participate in His Love by means of a unique spiritual relationship, i.e., His own Spirit indwelling the human spirit. But mankind sinned—rejected God's Love—and lost the special spiritual relationship with God. To remedy the situation, God sent His beloved Son to earth—oh, what Love!—to draw us unto Himself, that we might participate in His triune community of love, both here on earth and in heaven.

"What, or where, is heaven?" one might ask. It could be said that heaven is where God is. God is equivalent to heaven, for heaven *is* the presence of God, the fullness of God's Love.

Heaven is filled with forgiven sinners … but remarkably, hell is also filled with forgiven sinners!

We are all sinners, and because of God's great Love for mankind, we have all been forgiven. By Jesus' death on the cross, every person ever born has been forgiven. BUT, in order to lay claim to that forgiveness, a person must *choose* to accept it.

All those who choose to accept God's Love and forgiveness will share the joy and peace of God forever, in the fullness of His Love, in heaven. All those who reject God's Love and forgiveness *sentence themselves* to hell.

Remember, God does not send anyone to hell.

Hell is the consequence—
the self-imposed consequence—
of a person's decision not to choose God.

Heaven takes center stage in the Divine Drama of Love. God is there, surrounded by all those who have chosen to accept His Love and forgiveness and to participate in a love relationship with Him. They will join in the eternal love party in heaven.

Over on an obscure side stage is hell, the place reserved for those who have rejected God's Love and forgiveness. God is there too, for God is omnipresent (i.e., everywhere, all at the same time), but there is no partying going on in hell. Hell is when you know there's a grand party going on in heaven and that you were invited … but you permanently declined the invitation. Who would want to be an off-stage observer of the divine love party forever?

The invitation is extended to all. Have you accepted God's Love and forgiveness? Have you chosen God? If not, do so today! Come and take your place as a loving participant in the Divine Drama of Love.

* * * * *

Recommended Reading

In the interest of making this book a non-scholastic drama reading, I chose not to include footnotes. Below is a brief bibliography of some of the books I consulted while writing this book. They are recommended for your reading pleasure.

The original "spark" for developing this drama motif came from John Eldredge's book entitled *The Sacred Romance*, from chapter 6, "God the Ageless Romancer".

Buechner, Frederick, *Telling the Truth: The Gospel as Tragedy, Comedy, and Fairy Tale*. San Francisco: Harper Collins. 1977.

Capon, Robert Farrar, *The Mystery of Christ ... And Why We Don't Get It*. Grand Rapids: William B. Eerdmans Publ. 1993.

Edwards, Gene, *The Divine Romance: The Most Beautiful Love Story Ever Told*. Gardiner: Christian Books Publishing House. 1984.

Eldredge, John & Curtis, Brent, *The Sacred Romance: Drawing Closer to the Heart of God*. Nashville: Thomas Nelson Publishers. 1997.

Eldredge, John, *The Journey of Desire: Searching for the Life We've Only Dreamed Of*. Nashville: Thomas Nelson Publishers. 2000.

Kreeft, Peter, *Everything You Ever Wanted to Know about Heaven, but Never Dreamed of Asking!* San Francisco: Ignatius Press. 1990.

Kreeft, Peter, *Heaven: The Heart's Deepest Longing*. San
    Francisco: Ignatius Press. 1989.
Kruger, C. Baxter, *The Great Dance: The Christian Vision
    Revisited*. Jackson, MS: Perichoresis Press. 2000.
Lewis, Clyde Staples, *Mere Christianity*. New York:
    Macmillan Publishing. 1978.
Lewis, Clyde Staples, *The Great Divorce*. New York:
    Macmillan Publishing. 1946.